Travelers With No Ticket Home

OTHER BOOKS BY MARY MACKEY

Poetry

Sugar Zone, Marsh Hawk Press
Breaking The Fever, Marsh Hawk Press
The Dear Dance of Eros, Fjord Press
Skin Deep, Gallimaufry Press
One Night Stand, Effie's Press
Split Ends, Ariel Press

Novels

The Widow's War, Berkley Books
The Notorious Mrs. Winston, Berkley Books
The Year The Horses Came, Harper San Francisco
The Horses At the Gate, Harper San Francisco
The Fires of Spring, Penguin
Season of Shadows, Bantam
The Kindness of Strangers, Simon & Schuster
A Grand Passion, Simon & Schuster
The Last Warrior Queen, Putnam
McCarthy's List, Doubleday
Immersion, Shameless Hussy Press

Mary Mackey

Travelers
With
No Ticket
Home

poems by Mary Mackey

Winner of the 2012 PEN
Oakland Josephine Miles Award

MARSH HAWK PRESS
East Rockaway
2014

14 15 16 17 18   7 6 5 4 3 2 1   First Edition

Marsh Hawk Press books are published by Poetry Mailing List, Inc., a not-for-profit corporation under section 501 (c) 3 of the United States Internal Revenue Code.

Cover and Author Photo credit: Angus Wright
Cover Design: Claudia Carlson
Book set in Garamond Premiere Pro. and Californian for titles.

Publication of this book was supported by a generous grant from the Council of Literary Magazines and Presses via the New York State Council on the Arts.

Library of Congress Cataloging-in-Publication Data

Mackey, Mary.
  [Poems. Selections]
  Travelers with no ticket home : poems / by Mary Mackey.
    pages cm
  "Winner of the 2012 PEN Oakland Josephine Miles Award."
  Includes bibliographical references.
  ISBN 978-0-9882356-5-6 (pbk)
  I. Title.
  PS3563.A3165A6 2014
  811'.54--dc23
                          2014003635

Marsh Hawk Press
P.O. Box 206
East Rockaway, NY 11518-0206
www.marshhawkpress.org

Marsh
Hawk
Press

for A.W.

Contents

Preface • *ix*

1. Painted Tiger

Jacob's Ladder   *3*

Chacruna Traz Luz / Chacruna Brings Light   *4*

After Carnival   *5*

Saudade / Longing   *6*

Inquisition   *7*

A Estação das Chuvas / Rainy Season   *8*

Four Horses / *Quatro cavalos*   *9*

The Invisible Forests of Amapá   *10*

Amazonas   *11*

Under the Bocurubu Trees   *12*

The Wild Horses of Amazonas   *13*

Onça Pintada / Painted Tiger   *14*

Os Perdidos / The Lost Ones   *15*

Crown of Parrots   *16*

Cannibals   *17*

Conquistador   *18*

2. The City of Apocalyptic Visions

View from the Balcony   *21*

Travelers With No Ticket Home   *22*

Rio +3 Degrees / *Rio +3 graus*   *23*

The Welcoming Committee   *24*

Corcovado   *26*

Malaria / Dengue / Man-Moth / *Homen-traça*   *27*

Coriolis Effect / *Efeito Coriolis*   *28*

Fado of Two Lovers / *Fado de Dois Amantes*   *29*

Weather Report   *30*

The Reef   *31*

Chuva de Pedras / Rain of Stones   *32*

The People of Brazil Discover the Portuguese   *33*

Vidigal   *34*

Where I Left You   *35*

Boa Constrictor   *36*

The City of Apocalyptic Visions   *37*

Outside the Garden / *Fora do jardim*   *38*

3. Thornlands

Defective Instructions for Becoming a Shaman   *41*

Solange Encourages a River to Destroy a Dam   *42*

Solange Taunts the Colonels of Pará   *43*

Black Water / *Água Preta*   *44*

Caatinga / Thornlands   *45*

Nightingales   *46*

Milking the *Surucucu*   *47*

Mist Nets   *48*

Under The Cottonwoods   *49*

4. Language Lessons

In Those Days Rivers Could Not Cool Me   *53*

In the House of the Dead   *54*

March Floods / *Águas de Março*   *55*

Dreaming of the Dead We Have Loved   *56*

Under A Yellow Porch Light   *57*

Language Lessons / *Aulas de Idioma*   *58*

To My Mother on Her Second Non-Birthday   *59*

Iemanjá   *60*

5. The Kama Sutra of Kindness

Walking Toward the *Largo do Machado*   *63*

The Kama Sutra of Kindness: Position Number 1   *64*

The Kama Sutra of Kindness: Position Number 2   *65*

The Kama Sutra of Kindness: Position Number 3   *67*

The Kama Sutra of Kindness: Position Number 4   *70*

The Kama Sutra of Kindness: Position Number 5   *71*

The Kama Sutra of Kindness: Position Number 6   *72*

6. Traveler With No Ticket Home

The Martyrdom of Carmen Miranda   *75*

Notes   *77*

Acknowledgments   *79*

About the Author   *80*

Preface

Although about a third of the poems in this collection contain Portuguese words and phrases, the English-only portions are complete poems in themselves. They stand alone and can be read as if they were written solely in English. On the other hand, speakers of Portuguese will find subtle levels of meaning contained in the Portuguese phrases which enhance and deepen the poems. This interlingual collection continues my efforts to weave together two remarkably rich languages into poetry that is seamless, musical, and global.

1. Painted Tiger

Jacob's Ladder

my great aunts   hair done up in braids
calico feedsack dresses   aprons full of chicken feed
knew absolute silence   breath of a candle
hiss of a coal oil lamp   the cackle of a laying hen
but what would they have said
if I had spoken to them in Portuguese?

queridas tias / dearest aunts   the jungle is thicker than corn
mais grosso do que o milho
greener than cucumbers / *mais verde do que pepinos*
filled with black lagoons that shine like obsidian

queridas tias / dearest aunts
sooner or later / *mais cedo ou mais tarde*
we all stand at the foot of a ladder that's missing rungs
speaking in tongues no one can understand

Chacruna Traz Luz / Chacruna Brings Light

I still have that photo of you standing on the bank
of the Juruá   naked   your hair tangled
your lips pursed in surprise   or perhaps terror

On either side of you   wearing only penis gourds
two Kashinahua (or maybe Tarauacá) are blowing
hallucinogenic snuff up your nostrils
either through hollow puma bones
or the leg bones of some small bird   now extinct
whose feathers you have woven into the wreath
you wear as a crown

on the back of the photo you wrote:
Chacruna traz luz/Chacruna brings light
Huaira, Punga Amarillo, Capirona, Lopuna Blanca,
Challucahaki, Camu camu

the head spirits are starting to speak
my body is dissolving

and then   in an almost indecipherable scrawl:
get me out of here!

After Carnival

how you loved it in the beginning
the flashing sequins   the bare thighs and breasts
the drumming that you said made you feel
as if you were being passed from hand to hand
over a crowd of 72,000 people
who loved you more than your own mother

on Ash Wednesday everyone else stopped dancing
but you went on and on   as if someone had glued
invisible red shoes to your feet

even when it started raining and your feathers drooped
like the plumage of a dying bird
even when your purple wig bled into your eyes
and the soles of your feet were bloody
with the stigmata of your martyrdom
you kept on chanting the name of Yansan
Candomblé goddess of wind and storms
merciless Yansan who rode you like a horse
and pulled on your legs and arms with invisible strings

the samba whispers terrible secrets!
you cried but you would not tell me what they were

how easy it is to give ourselves to the gods, *o meu bem*
how hard to take ourselves back

Saudade / Longing

in this vine-tangled forest
in this jungle that lures us into its snares
we long for wide meadows   leafless trees   purple shadows
that run in the gullies like spilled wine

when did we lose the silence of long winter nights
broken only by the sting of snow
the flight of white owls   the snapping of twigs
the hiss of our skates moving down creeks
over schools of fish   frozen beneath us
like souls trapped between two worlds

Inquisition

You ask me how I am
pecking like a yellow-tailed cuckoo
at the thin shield of green heat
that protects me from a sky that can be shredded like paper

in this land   god is a poisonous spider
the size of a shoe   a lash of fire ants
a snake with hinged fangs

above this tangled canopy of doomed trees
the clouds are writing desperately important messages
we can't read   and that log lodged in the mud behind you
is an alligator with teeth like a cross-cut saw

do not ask me how I am
do not ask me if we will survive

there are so many ways to die here
I've lost track

A Estação das Chuvas / Rainy Season

suspended on a black mirror that reflects the sky
we pass our fingers through clouds
as if they were the souls of birds

this river   sixty-five feet in flood
has lifted us to the tops of the trees
now we are drifting   too exhausted to speak
afraid to break the silence that holds us together

Four Horses / *Quatro cavalos*

We saw four horses swimming
their tails floating out behind them
como correntes pretas
the sun breaking on the
ripples of their breath
like shattered gold

The Invisible Forests of Amapá

Crested Capuchin, Nectar Bat,
Three-toed Sloth, Golden Lion Tamarin,
Red-Handed Howling Monkey, Dark-Throated
Seedeater, Blue-Winged Macaw

great rivers veiled in steam
sixty billion trees
reaching toward a sky so green
it burns like copper

Amazonas

we walk on the bottom of an invisible ocean
under us the ground heaves in slow waves

look   the masts of a thousand   ten thousand   a million
sunken ships   surround us in a cage of pale flame

over our heads vast green clouds tremble in the dying light
the Waiká have warned us to be silent
they say if we open our mouths here
we will drown

Under the Bocurubu Trees

When the river twisted east like a streamer of honed silver
and flocks of macaws burned blue in the *bocurubu* trees
the last six speakers of *Arikapú*
walked through shadows hot as cooling iron
whispering to each other in a language that sounded
like water running over pebbles

they did not turn to look at us   standing there beside our canoes
we were the noise that had drowned their silence
the thieves who had cut out their tongues
pale ghosts in their green light
our words harsh and incomprehensible
as the ringing of axes

The Wild Horses of Amazonas

the trees were a herd of giant horses standing over us
their manes blowing in the wind

you said   *all this belongs to us*
and we belong to it

Onça Pintada / Painted Tiger

at night when we wake   we see Solange standing beside us
and feel *seu hálito quente* / her hot breath
on our faces

trees and vines are tattooed on her body
when she moves   they flow across her breasts and thighs
como o Rio Branco em inundação
like the Rio Solimões in flood

Solange   who stalks us by day
and watches over us by night
Solange   who is everything we have destroyed

Castanha-de-cutia, castanha-do-pará,
angelim-vermelho
the lungs of the world emptied
its rivers fouled with arsenic

Solange   *a única que é tudo*
the painted tiger who pads behind us
on soft paws

Os Perdidos / **The Lost Ones**

Nós somos os perdidos,   We are the lost ones
os que não podem   the ones who can't find the path
encontrar o caminho.
               —Heloisa Santos

in the green heat of the south
we long for snow   imagine
inconceivable things   mittens
the ache of frost
always wanting to be where we aren't
always longing to return to the place we just left
refugees from a disaster we can't name

somewhere along the way
we have lost everything that tells us who we are
now we stand on the banks of a dark river
in front of a hollow tree   inside
a cauldron of bats with milk-stained breasts
is singing us deaf

Crown of Parrots

Among the pale columns of light
that fall from the great trees
wild pigs are swimming the river
like commuters entering a phantom city

your breath smells of *pinga*
your lips are the color of *açaí*
the forest floor beneath our feet
seethes with iridescent flies
that rise up around us in clouds like hissing stars

you are calling up the dead again
the lost ones who leave holes at our tables
chanting in that high, terrifying voice you
always used when you spoke to your mother

Seru, Guanandi, Conduru   you are crying
there will be no escape
Pau-marfim, Angelim-Vermelho, Crown of Parrots

Solange, what horrors are you courting
as we stand knee-deep in flies
trapped between this black-water river
and this muddy *igarapé*

Cannibals

É preciso escolher um caminho que não tenha fim.
—TARSILA DO AMARAL

strangler figs snaked
toward a cut-lemon sun
the trunks of the Cedro-Faias
flickered like a cage of sea-green flames

above us   a troop of black-capped capuchins
slept   draped over the limbs
of the Jequitibá-Rosa like wet, brown rags

we had lived our lives all wrong
betrayed everything we cherished
gone at each other like spitting pit vipers

now we lay together in one hammock
forced into forgiveness
dreaming of snow   bitter winds
air thin enough to breathe

Conquistador

on the far side of the lagoon
he rides in circles

day after day he follows the same path
searching for a way back to the mountains
where the air is cold and clear
and the snow burns his flesh like frozen iron

he came to this place to conquer it
but how do you conquer mud and water
birds so bright they burn your eyes
women who can walk through trees
men whose arrows stop your breath

once he wanted to rule a continent
now all he wants is to find
four square feet of dirt
solid enough to stand on

2. The City of Apocalyptic Visions

View from the Balcony

Nine times the sun rose over the bay
nine times the sea looked as if some great
fish had been slaughtered between
the channel and the point

in the streets people dressed in strange
brightly-colored clothing
danced to songs of drought and starvation

each night the spirit of Elizabeth Bishop
walked in the park her lover had designed
where palm trees waved like human hands
the wind was a cough that stopped and started
and the heat burned like strong coffee

from our balcony high above it all
we could see long white ships
taking people to kinder places

this is how we learned about despair
this is how we were schooled in it

Travelers With No Ticket Home

nesta cidade dos sonhos
in this city of hallucinations
the air is like *cola quente* / hot glue
and the buildings are stuck waist-deep
in asphalt *tão suave* / so soft
you can chew it like gum

over the sea the frigate birds hang motionless
parados   congeladas
stopped in mid-flight like a flock of ethereal scissors

in the parks *acima da cidade*
hikers are ambushed
and robbed at gunpoint
by hungry men in rubber sandals
who flow out of a jungle thick as green glass

on some days in mid-summer
no meio do verão
when the heat seethes off the pavement
like steam   and the moon is waxing left to right
and water is swirling slowly down the drains
in the wrong direction
and the hospitals are full of
children crucified
by breakbone fever

the newly resurrected join us
and we wander the streets together
eating spoiled shrimp and drinking warm beer

Rio +3 Degrees / Rio +3 graus

every evening / *cada crepúsculo* dusk falls
like burning oil blurring the stoplights
and lacquering the streets with a haze
that smells of gardenias and *açaí*

around us the apartments of Catete rise
como colunas de fumaça / like columns of smoke
their windows shining like the blades
of newly sharpened knives

we are skirting puddles slapping mosquitoes
evitando carros dodging cars
walking over the graves of trees through a jungle of ghosts
toward a future we can't imagine

we know something has gone terribly wrong
yet we argue bitterly over trivial things

when at last we stop
to buy sticks of flavored ice to cool our throats
they melt before we can taste them

The Welcoming Committee

I conceive there is more barbarity in tearing a [man's] body limb from limb
by racks and torments . . . under the color of piety and religion, than to roast
and eat him after he is dead.

—MICHEL DE MONTAIGNE, *On Cannibals*

behind the mountains   lies another range of mountains
made of clouds   where the dead rock in hammocks
woven of snakes

and behind that lies a fire that never stops burning
and behind that still more mountains
made of a smoke that sears our lungs
like burned sugar

the air here is clear and thick as gelatin
and everything trapped in it is dead
poised forever above a sea of molten glass

we are birds with black wings
that have been sewn on our backs
by our enemies (of which we have many)

we can smell the dust on high cabinets
mites in our clothing
cats on the street eleven stories below us

our throats are made of clay
our livers are on fire
we are blind and clairvoyant

we are the Portuguese coming into Guanabara Bay
in caravels after eight months
of fucking each other and eating rats

we are fools and scoundrels
saints and sadists

we are two lovers in an apartment
enclosed in glass

we are everyone and no one

we are the Portuguese coming into Guanabara Bay
waving at the beautiful naked people on the beach
who are waiting to eat us

Corcovado

You said the boy god   *o menino deus*
who spreads his arms over this city
was finished   *terminado, liquidado, acabado*
and that you wanted to hear nothing more
of holy men with holes in their sides
and blood on their hands

when the dancers came
stamping their bare feet in the wet sand
you joined them   grabbed handfuls of white roses
and threw them into the sea

they only walked in up to their waists
but you went all the way under
down into *o vidro quebrado*, broken glass,
and slick sewage of 40 favelas

when you finally came up
you had become a shark-skinned goddess
an eel-tongued Medusa
with all the oceans of the world
tangled in your hair

Malaria / Dengue / Man-Moth / *Homem-traça*

rains swept the streets
washing hallucinations into the sewers
on the soccer field   under lights that cut the
night to shreds   the games went on

you lay on a narrow cot   in a small room
drinking rum   picking at the sheets
and reciting scraps of poetry

geckos ate the mosquitoes on the walls
blackflies swarmed around the lamp
the water tasted like mold
the floors buckled   gunfire rattled in the distance
and the sirens never stopped keening

just before dawn   you told me you could see stairs made of fever
don't climb them! I begged   but as always you ignored me

you're a coward   you said   *you know nothing of beauty*
Elizabeth Bishop herself is standing here
with one arm around Lota   and the other around the Man-Moth

Homem-traça
Homem-traça
doesn't that mean anything to you!

then you begged me to help you
beat your hands against the sides of your cot
clawed at your eyes

Coriolis Effect / *Efeito Coriolis*

machinegun fire tapping on the walls
chips of plaster falling from the ceiling
out in the streets / *nas ruas abaixo de nós*
people are dying

we sit in the shower fully clothed
plunging our fingers into the soapy water
forcing it to go right   forcing it to go left
watching the drain suck it down

tonight we are drunk on terror
how long can we sit here
quanto tempo podemos ficar
before we choke on the bones
of a fear too thick to swallow

Fado of Two Lovers / *Fado de Dois Amantes*

Quando cantamos fados,   When we sing fados
cantamos da crueldade do destino.   we sing of the cruelty of fate.
Cantamos dos amantes que perdemos   We sing of the lovers we have lost,
os amigos que nunca veremos outra vez   the friends we'll never see again.

—LUIZ ÁLVARES, FROM *O MUNDO MELANCOLIA DE FADO*

our future is a river of dust that disappears into a desert
our past   scars tattooed on our flesh one half-forgotten night
when we got drunk and went under the needle

we came here as gods   walking on broken glass
trailing auras of fire

now we lie back to back
eyes shut   fists clenched
wondering which of us will betray the other   first

Weather Report

down on the beach we are scooping sand into
our mouths   hoping to speak in tongues
but every grain scours us dumb

on the horizon we can see the hurricane
coming back like a mad dancer
with one blind eye

we have heard there are people who cut off
their fingers to mourn the dead
but we don't have enough fingers
between the two of us to do the job

The Reef

sea fan, rose lace, blade fire, feather
blushing star, elkhorn, ten-ray, brain

deserted as a cathedral on Good Friday
when the lamps have been extinguished
and the altar draped in black
drowned in water so clear it looks like glass
the ghost corals glitter beneath us like the ruins of ancient cities
annealed to alabaster by some inconceivable calamity

Chuva de Pedras / Rain of Stones

an empty sky
a crescent beach smeared with salt water warm as blood
quem poderia ter previsto who could have foreseen
that rain of stones or how bitterly
we would accuse each other

as we raged and swore *maluco! doida! safado!*
villages were being buried in ash
wells were vomiting fire
children were choking on air the color of old plastic

but we were *teimosos e estúpidos*
young and unhappy
we could not imagine
mountains exploding birds struck down in flight
pain inflicted without intention

The People of Brazil Discover the Portuguese

Easter, April 1, 1500

Vast blue bleeding into a gray horizon
surf choking on the rocks
something has broken through the storm clouds
that line up in the afternoon like bundles of piassava

for thousands of years we have had our canoes,
our fishing nets circling in the air
the taste of mangos in our mouths
the rocking of our hammocks
the scent of jacaranda

what is it that comes out of the east
like a tower of bones
white   with fluttering wings
larger than the largest bird we have ever seen

what new plague is the wind
blowing toward us

Vidigal

on the sweeping crescent of sand
that embraces the sea   sweat rises
from the backs of sunbathers
like a flight of souls

as we climb up to the favela of Vidigal
each flight of steps ends in a burst of light
a blank wall   an abandoned car   a cobbled street
a raft of litter and bougainvillea

in the nursery school   in the building
drug dealers once occupied
two-year-olds are dying eggs
eating carrot cake   making Easter bunnies
from popcorn and white paper

above them   close as breath
in the room where the gang used to cremate the bodies
of the men they murdered   there is a small chapel
consecrated to the memory of the dead
where two candles sit in tin holders
in front of a plaster Virgin

below   the children laugh and crack open colored eggs
sheltered beneath a cloak of invisible ashes
and unspoken sorrows

Where I Left You

In this city where the buildings are rotted with mold
in this city of our abandoned bodies
where the streets are paved with glass

in this city of despair where the poor live
in cardboard packing crates and children
are born to be shot

here   right here   is where I left you
slumped up against a wall
sullen with a grief you refused to share

Boa Constrictor

when the heat pounds like a hammer
and every shadow is a glowing anvil
I can feel your body again   pressed against mine
long   cool   and coiling

I want to fight with you
explain all those things
you would never let me explain
but you have gone to live in your land of thorns
where the horses wear coats of leather

in this wind that gives no relief
I hear your breath smooth as molten sand
scouring my throat

I imagine you hovering over me   listening to my heart
waiting for it to stop beating
but except for the black-caged fan
that whirls above me like a giant insect
nothing in this room moves   but slow suffocation

The City of Apocalyptic Visions

Broken windows   stops in a giant
harmonica wailing in the hot winds that blow
up from the South   and you again in this room
with the broken lamp and the sprung bed
floating half an inch above my carpet
with your eyes closed and your lips drawn back

my love   my yellow-eyed jaguar
I am not the one who is dead
you are   and yet you return
chewing on coca leaves
drinking guarana   feeding on my
bitterness and remorse as if they were sugar

You come back unbidden to tell your endless stories
of black rivers   wild pigs   spiders big as saucers
red-eyed monkeys that fuck in the trees
better than you/better than you ever could

Solange   if you are dead
stay that way   stay in that half-forgotten jungle
that rises off my life like pale steam
don't visit me here in this city you hated
its streets   its sewers   its long hard winters
its dirt   grit   absence of stars

In the end you even hated my body
which you said had come to smell like civilization
how bitterly you said that word
as if your tongue were the tongue
of a fer-de-lance
as if everything except me
was green   tangled   too beautiful to bear

Outside the Garden / *Fora do jardim*

onde fica   where is that city with its bruised sky
endless soccer games
buildings dripping with rust and rot
air blued with the scent of bananas and mold
people who dance when there is no reason for joy

onde ficam / where are   those long nights
densas, quentes, e úmidas
walls drenched in jasmine and piss
silent parks where bands of monkeys sleep in Jabuticaba trees
and malaria burns off the puddles like black fire

here in the cold lands the wind is blowing from the north
our gardens are dying   the earth is hardening
and naked twigs are whipping at our windows like headless snakes

3. Thornlands

Defective Instructions For Becoming a Shaman

cast off your flesh like the pelt of a molting snake   you told me
walk to the *aldeia dos mortos* / the village of the dead
where the old grow young   the young grow old
and women hunt jaguars under a snake of stars

become *um morcego*   a bat
an armadillo   a bird with a human face
não pode haver nada no mundo que não é você
there can be nothing left in the world that isn't you

you never mentioned the web that hangs between
the visible and invisible worlds
dancers who hold their eyes in their hands
the *Boitatá* who glows in the dark
the *Mapinguari* who rips the tongues from cows
the *Curupira* who eats poachers

you didn't warn me about *o túnel de espinhos*
the river of snakes   the plain of thorns
or those transparent beings with small hot hands
who would offer me a crown of Macaw feathers

now I sit here   trapped in the curare of regret
as fever eats my body like a hungry *jacaré*

Solange Encourages a River to Destroy a Dam

Xingu   Xingu
who is that dancer whirling and blind
Xingu   what god rides her head

Xingu you are a *jagunço*   a *jararaca*
uma santa mulher   a holy woman
who smokes a cigar

you are the *boca da cobra*   the mouth of the snake
the soft pink part we see just before it strikes

Solange Taunts The Colonels of Pará

She lifts the flowers to her lips and blows on them
until the petals flap like the wings of egrets
she disappears becomes invisible incorporeal immaterial/delusional
transforms herself into a snake   stalks us like a jaguar
tears out our throats and heals us with a kiss

when the colonels and their *jagunços* come to kill her
she greets them by pulling up her skirt
which of you fat men with big guns and small pistolas
is brave enough to enter the door that leads nowhere   she cries
which of you wants to die with the taste of cashews on his tongue?

after they run away   she sleeps for forty days
when she wakes   she tells us to place another row
of small black seeds on her tongue   calls them
the bitter stones that pave the path to Paradise

Black Water / *Água Preta*

Rio Negro   Rio Negro
rio de água preta   blackwater river
três mil peixes que   three thousand fish
podemos comer   we can eat
seis que nos comem   six that can eat us

    —Cléa Abreu

The forest was a green dome
the water an ebony mirror
we saw ourselves floating between two worlds
both made of sky

our guide had lost a leg to a *jararaca*
when you threw yourself into the river   he wept
warned you of *candirus*, piranhas, stingrays
enguias elétricas that could fuse your spine like wire

but you came up laughing
to tell us that two great *arapaimas*
had slipped between your thighs like silk ribbons

they entered your brain   you said
swam inside your skull   showed you a country
where all the fish were made of stained glass
and all the windows paned with silver scales

you claimed you had dived to the bottom where the *jaú* sleep
sunk into mud   solitude   peace
said   when you looked up and saw the soles of our feet
you pitied us for not being able to breathe water

Caatinga / Thornlands

In a thorn canyon *em um barranco de espinhos*
beside brackish water
ankle-deep in dust that burned our throats
sob um céu claro implacável
under a relentlessly clear sky filled with crawling shadows
you put your hands over my eyes

imagine nothing you said *remember nothing
lembrar de nada*

but I could see light streaming through your palms
feel the heat of your breath
taste the salt on your fingers

Nightingales

In the dying light   when the grapes
hung heavy   and the owls hunted   and all the small things
in the darkness did not know the names we had given them
I saw you again   reincarnated as a black horizon

saw the whipsaw of your smile   the dirt
under your fingernails   the way you threw back
your head when you laughed   your disdain
for joy

that night (and that night only)   I smelled the hot scent
of your flesh as if we still stood arguing in that forest
where once   long ago   the howler monkeys taunted us
like insane nightingales

Milking the *Surucucu*

We stood face to face sweating
and slapping at blackflies
and fought about the best way
to milk a snake for its venom

you had just caught a *surucucu* behind the neck
nine feet long a head a handspan across
already it was coiling up your arm
as if the rainforest had come alive on your flesh

your eyes were closed   your head was back
your lips were pursed   as if waiting for a kiss

I often think of how you dreamed of death, Solange
how relentlessly you pursued it

Mist Nets

Mist nets / *redes de neblina*   made of human hair
billowing like waves of luminous dust
dividing the jungle into windows / *janelas* / *buracos*
the size of postage stamps

one by one the humming birds are trapped
small pulsing soap bubbles of red green gold
throats streaked with a blue so bright
tão brilhante, tão quente   so hot   so hopeless
it blinds like the tip of a dying match

every time they struggle to escape
cada vez que eles lutam para escapar
the threads wrap around them more tightly

sempre este querido   always this, my love
first the ecstatic flight   then the invisible snare

Under The Cottonwoods

leaves waver   rippled and striated
sand shifts in invisible currents
below us the water weeds are swaying
and the carp glow silver   look

when I hold up the palm of my hand
it has no substance
if I place it on your forehead
it will pass through to the
other side

we are not lovers any more
or even friends
we are only light on water

4. Language Lessons

In Those Days Rivers Could Not Cool Me

I once lived in places
where volcanoes erupted   the water was poison
and the night swarmed with termites
that tasted like glue

there were rooms where I lay so wrapped
in fever that the fans overhead seemed ecstatic
in their whirling
rooms where I saw light the color of blood and bruised
plums   had hallucinations   dreams   terrors so great
they set me shrieking

once for 4 hours straight I spoke in rhymed couplets
and no one could make me shut up
until I threw off the sheets and ran into the tropical night
like a woman on fire

in those days   rivers could not cool me
threats could not subdue me   I burned
and burned with illness   lust   and fear
and your lightest touch seemed like a blow

later   I cooked a monkey in cream sauce
and we ate it as jungle rats ran the rafters
over our heads   the next afternoon I nearly
stepped on a nine foot fer-de-lance

only a mad woman could have loved such a life
but I did   I do   loved the strangeness of it
the non-humanness of it   the sure knowledge that death
was so small and close it could buzz in my ear

In The House of the Dead

somewhere there is a baby crying
somewhere   the sound of glass breaking
somewhere   the moan of wind through a half-open door

here you search for the people you love
and fear to find them

March Floods / *Águas de Março*

we found you caught in the lips of the delta
pequena e pálida / small and pale
a school of fish   snarled in your hair
like poisoned ribbons

Dreaming of the Dead We Have Loved

they move toward us slowly like swimmers
floating toward the top of a pool that has no surface

in the rooms they visit   all the clocks have stopped
and the windows have been thrown wide open

outside   vast fields stretch toward horizons without vanishing points
the trees are made of amber   the sky is cut glass
and the locusts in the corn are as big as tractors

when we sit down to eat our breakfasts
the dead sit across from us and try to attract our attention
they smile   speak   take our hands in theirs
we still love you   they say
we will always love you

but we the living are always too busy eating to notice
our cereal is getting soggy   our tea is getting cold
we greet the dead casually without looking up
take back our hands   pick up our spoons

Under A Yellow Porch Light

Naquela terra perdida e esquecida,   In that lost and forgotten land
os mortos são ressuscitados   the dead are resurrected

— HELOISA SANTOS

all I want is an ordinary evening with them
an evening when they are alive and solid
sweating and laughing and smelling of coffee and smoke

just an hour with them on the front porch
in the heat of summer   in a creaking swing
the sound of cards slapping down on cement steps

the leaves of the sugar maples moving like heat-drugged ghosts
fireflies hanging above the peonies like votive candles
a child skating in and out of the shadows of a streetlight

a few houses away   someone will call out a name
and under a yellow porch light
in a country that no longer appears on any map
on a continent surrounded by a sea filled with dragons
the ordinary nothing that is everything will go on

Language Lessons / *Aulas de idioma*

in his old age   my father became a master of forgetting
not *truck! truck!* but *big thing! big thing!*
spoken not like a child but like an intelligent stranger
trying to communicate in a language
he had studied long ago

I once swallowed something that made me forget
what I held in my hand
I stared at it in dumb admiration   *aturdida, extasiada*
seeing in its depths the entrance to another world

at last   I opened my fingers
sure it would float in front of me like a new planet

there was a crash, a *baque*, an *estrondo*
and a shower of small shards rose up from the linoleum
like a fountain of green stars

To My Mother On Her Second Non-Birthday

My years are no longer measured
in months and days
they're measured in how long it's been
since I last saw you

I can never make myself believe our parting was final
I feel as if you are hiding somewhere
waiting to spring out and surprise me when I least expect it

some morning my phone will ring
some afternoon you will knock on my door
some evening you will come in   take off your coat
and sit down

we will have nothing much to say to each other
as we drink our coffee   yet that almost nothing
will be more than enough

Iemanjá

Afro-Brazilian Goddess of the Sea

By day the foam curls under her feet
like a carpet of broken crystals

by night she moves beneath the waves
dark-skinned mother
glowing mystery of the deepest rifts
she who climbs mountains
that have never seen the sun

in her left hand she holds a mirror
that reflects your face
as it would have appeared
if you had drowned

your eyes swimming in your head
like a pair of startled fish
your lashes trembling like seaweed
your lips wet and open
all your pain dissolved in her salty kisses

5. The Kama Sutra of Kindness

Walking toward the *Largo do Machado*

when the smell of jasmine
flows through the streets of Catete like a warm fog
when the scent is so liquid you can
breathe it in   get drunk and stagger
I think of all the years I have loved you
and all the years I will go on loving you
I think of how we protect each other from pain and betrayal
how each night we wrap ourselves around each other
and peace floats above our bed like a canopy of white petals

The Kama Sutra of Kindness: Position Number 1

in ancient Japan
after the first night
poems were exchanged
between lovers

a branch of white blossoms
rests against the sky
you sleep
on my blue silk sheets

the brush brings words
to the blank rice papers
you touch me
and I speak

the third time
you enter a woman
it is mandatory
to say something kind

when I smell your hair
I think of wind and anemone

the imagination has
its own erogenous zones

your body bears me
to another season
thank you for resting
here with me
balanced on the crested moon

(from *The Dear Dance of Eros,* 1987)

The Kama Sutra of Kindness: Position Number 2

should I greet you
as if
we had merely eaten
together one night
when the white birches
dripped wet
and lightning etched
black trees on your walls?

it is not love
I am asking

love comes from years
of breathing
skin to skin
tangled in each other's dreams
until each night
weaves another thread
in the same web
of blood and sleep

    and I have only
    passed though you quickly
    like light
    and you have only
    surrounded me suddenly
    like flame

the lake is cold
the snows are sudden
the wild cherry bends
and winter's a burden

in your hand I feel
spring burn in the bud

(from *The Dear Dance of Eros,* 1987)

The Kama Sutra of Kindness: Position Number 3

It's easy to love
through a cold spring
when the poles
of the willows
turn green
pollen falls like
a yellow curtain
and the scent of
Paper Whites
clots
the air

but to love for a lifetime
takes talent

you have to mix yourself
with the strange
beauty of someone
else
wake each morning
for 72,000
mornings in
a row so
breathed and
bound and
tangled
that you can hardly
sort out
your arms
and
legs

you have to
find forgiveness
in everything
even ink stains
and broken
cups

you have be willing to move through
life
together
the way the long
grasses move
in a field
when you careen
blindly toward
the other
side

there's never going to be anything
straight or predictable
about your path
except the
flattening
and the springing
back

you just go on walking for years
hand in hand
waist deep in the weeds
bent slightly forward
like two question
marks
and all the while it

burns
my dear
it burns beautifully above
you
and goes on
burning
like a relentless
sun

(from *Breaking The Fever*, 2006)

The Kama Sutra of Kindness: Position Number 4

you claim you long for me   the way
a drowning man longs to breathe

poised above me   tortured as a saint
you pause then descend   speaking
with a tongue that tastes of honey
and salt

reason be damned

look
even the light around us has
changed

(from *Sugar Zone*, 2011)

The Kama Sutra of Kindness: Position Number 5

in the flame
of a single candle   entire cities
   are appearing
   and disappearing

my hands tremble on you
my fingers pass through you
your tongue tastes like apples
your flesh is fog

above our roof the jealous moon
has torn a hole in the sky

(from *Sugar Zone*, 2011)

The Kama Sutra of Kindness: Position Number 6

a river of molten glass paved with fine white sand
and on the far bank   a thousand trees eternally burning
eternally throwing themselves into the sky

look   we are two blue-winged macaws
frozen in mid-flight over a wall of green fire
strangers lost in the jungle of each other's bodies
lovers who don't want to be found

6. Traveler With No Ticket Home

The Martyrdom of Carmen Miranda

If you want to look like the quintessential hoochie coochie girl, there
is no better costume to have than the Ultimate Collection Carmen Miranda Outfit.
—RUBIE'S COSTUME COMPANY, ADVERTISEMENT

in that foreign land
you were always a joke
the fruit basket hats
the crippling high heels
the bare midriff
the broken English
the carnival mask smile

done up in pompoms like a pet poodle
wearing your past on the inside
like a hair shirt
the Brazilian Bombshell
who could only say *hot dog*
moneey moneey moneey
does you like me?

never mentioning
the long hours you worked in the hat shop
to buy medicine for your tubercular sister
the bad marriage to the man who beat you
the miscarriages, depression, pills
the pain you felt when at last you came home
and discovered your own people despised you
for selling out to Uncle Sam

when your gay composer protested
your betrayal of Brazil by swallowing rat poison
you danced on like a frantic puppet
singing of the Afro-Brazilian gods
in a language no one understood

Chica Chica Boom Chic
Chica Chica Boom Chic

Carmen   like you we are all travelers
who set out believing we can bring back
something to make it worth the trip
money, love, hammocks, fame
something that will make us happy and whole
something that will heal our wounds
and give us peace

Notes

Jacob's Ladder: Jacob's Ladder is a traditional quilt pattern. It is also the ladder to Heaven the biblical Jacob dreams about as described in *Genesis* 28: 10-19.

Chacruna Traz Luz / Chacruna Brings Light: Chacruna (*Psychotria viridis*) is one of the ingredients of the psychoactive drink ayahuasca (also known as yagé) used for divinatory and healing purposes by the native peoples of the Amazon. The composition of ayahuasca was first formally described in the 1950s by Harvard Ethnobotanist Richard Evans Schultes.

The Invisible Forests of Amapá: 90% of the total area of Brazilian state of Amapá is covered with Amazonian rainforest. About 70% of this forest has not been explored by non-indigenous people and thus remains unmapped. The state of Amapá possesses the lowest rate of loss of its original vegetation of any Brazilian state, estimated at present at only about 2%.

Under the Bocurubu Trees: As of 1998 there were only six surviving speakers of the Brazilian indigenous language *Arikapúi*.

Malaria / Dengue / Man-Moth / Homen-traça: this poem contains references to Elizabeth Bishop's poem *The Man-Moth*.

Fado of Two Lovers / Fado de Dois Amantes: Fados are Portuguese songs about loss and longing.

Solange Encourages a River to Destroy a Dam: the Xingu is a 1,200 mile Brazilian river that empties into the Amazon River. Brazil is planning the construction of a huge dam on the Xingu called Belo Monte. As the third-largest hydroelectric project in the world, Belo Monte would divert nearly the entire flow of the Xingu through two artificial canals leaving indigenous communities without water, fish, or means of river transport. Protests against Belo Monte are on-going. *Jagunço* is a one of 25 Brazilian Portuguese words for "hitman."

Mist Nets: Mist nets are used by biologists to capture wild birds or bats for research purposes. When put up properly they are virtually invisible. In the past mist nets were made of human hair. At present, most are made of nylon mesh.

Acknowledgments

Thanks to Dr. Lise Sedrez, Professor of History at the Instituto de História, Universidade Federal do Rio de Janeiro. Dr. Sedrez, born and reared in Rio de Janeiro, patiently and expertly proofread all the Portuguese words and phrases in this collection. Thanks also to Thomas Fink whose insightful editorial suggestions were invaluable and to Sandy McIntosh and Claudia Carlson who worked unstintingly to get *Travelers* ready for publication.

I am grateful to writers Dorothy Hearst and Pamela Berkman who gave me companionship and support during the writing of these poems as did members of The WELL, the women of Word of Mouth Bay Area and the San Francisco branch of the Women's National Book Association. Lastly, I want to thank my husband Angus Wright for sharing his knowledge of Brazil with me and for his unfailing affection and support; and the late Richard Evans Schultes, Harvard Professor and father of modern Ethnobotany, who generously allowed me to audit his classes where, as an eighteen-year-old sophomore, I first fell in love with the beauty and mystery of the tropics.

I wish to express my gratitude to the periodicals in which many of the poems in this collection first appeared: *Catamaran Literary Reader*: "*Onça Pintanda* / Painted Tiger"; *Gargoyle Magazine*: "Coriolus Effect," "Rio +3 Degrees / *Rio +3 graus*," "Inquisition"; *Marsh Hawk Review*: "View From the Balcony," "Cannibals," Travelers With No Ticket Home"; *Plume Poetry: An Online Journal*: "Jacob's Ladder," "In Those Days Rivers Could Not Cool Me," "Outside the Garden / *Fora do jardim*," "*Chacruna Traz Luz* / Chacruna Brings Light"; *Poetry Flash*: "After Carnival"; *Spillway*: "The City of Apocalyptic Visions," "Nightingales"; *The Understanding Between Foxes and Light*: "Solange Encourages A River to Destroy a Dam."

About the Author

Mary Mackey received her B. A. from Harvard and a Ph.D. in Comparative Literature from the University of Michigan. She is the author of six previous collections of poetry including *Sugar Zone* (Marsh Hawk Press, 2011) winner of the 2012 PEN Oakland Josephine Miles Award for Excellence in Literature. Her poems, which have appeared in many magazines and anthologies, have been praised by Wendell Berry, Jane Hirshfield, Dennis Nurkse, Ron Hanson, Al Young, and Marge Piercy for their beauty, precision, originality, and extraordinary range. Garrison Keillor has read her poetry four times on his show *The Writer's Almanac*.

She is also the author of thirteen novels, several of which have made *The New York Times* and *San Francisco Chronicle* bestseller lists. Her first novel *Immersion* (Shameless Hussy Press, 1972) is set in the rainforests of Costa Rica where Mackey lived in her twenties. Mackey's works have been translated into twelve foreign language including Japanese, Hebrew, Russian, Greek, and Finnish. She is past president of the West Coast branch of PEN, a Fellow of the Virginia Center for the Creative Arts, and Professor Emeritus of English at California State University, Sacramento. For the last twenty years she has been traveling to Brazil with her husband, Angus Wright, who writes about land reform and environmental issues.

To contact her, sample more of her work, and read her blog *The Writer's Journey*, you are invited to visit her website at http://www.marymackey.com. You can follow her on Twitter at @Mary_Mackey and find her on Facebook at https://www.facebook.com/marymackeywriter. Her books are available both in hard copy and as ebooks.

Titles From Marsh Hawk Press

Jane Augustine, *A Woman's Guide to Mountain Climbing, Night Lights, Arbor Vitae*

Thomas Beckett, ~~Dipstick~~/*Diptych*

Sigman Byrd, *Under the Wanderer's Star*

Patricia Carlin, *Quantum Jitters, Original Green*

Claudia Carlson, *Pocket Park, The Elephant House*

Meredith Cole, *Miniatures*

Neil de la Flor, *An Elephant's Memory of Blizzards, Almost Dorothy*

Chard deNiord, *Sharp Golden Thorn*

Sharon Dolin, *Serious Pink*

Steve Fellner, *The Weary World Rejoices, Blind Date with Cavafy*

Thomas Fink, *Joyride, Peace Conference, Clarity and Other Poems, After Taxes, Gossip: A Book of Poems*

Norman Finkelstein, *Inside the Ghost Factory, Passing Over*

Edward Foster, *Dire Straits, The Beginning of Sorrows, What He Ought To Know, Mahrem: Things Men Should Do for Men*

Paolo Javier, *The Feeling Is Actual*

Burt Kimmelman, *Somehow*

Burt Kimmelman and Fred Caruso, *The Pond at Cape May Point*

Basil King, *77 Beasts: Basil King's Bestiary, Mirage*

Martha King, *Imperfect Fit*

Phillip Lopate, *At the End of the Day: Selected Poems and An Introductory Essay*

Mary Mackey, *Travelers With No Ticket Home, Sugar Zone, Breaking the Fever*

Jason McCall, *Dear Hero,*

Sandy McIntosh, *Cemetery Chess: Selected and New Poems, Ernesta, in the Style of the Flamenco, Forty-Nine Guaranteed Ways to Escape Death, The After-Death History of My Mother, Between Earth and Sky*

Stephen Paul Miller, *There's Only One God and You're Not It, Fort Dad, The Bee Flies in May, Skinny Eighth Avenue*

Daniel Morris, *If Not for the Courage, Bryce Passage*

Sharon Olinka, *The Good City*

Justin Petropoulos, *Eminent Domain*

Paul Pines, *Last Call at the Tin Palace*

Jacquelyn Pope, *Watermark*

Karin Randolph, *Either She Was*

Rochelle Ratner, *Ben Casey Days, Balancing Acts, House and Home*

Michael Rerick, *In Ways Impossible to Fold*

Corrine Robins, *Facing It: New and Selected Poems, Today's Menu, One Thousand Years*

Eileen R. Tabios, *The Thorn Rosary: Selected Prose Poems and New (1998–2010), The Light Sang As It Left Your Eyes: Our Autobiography, I Take Thee, English, for My Beloved, Reproductions of the Empty Flagpole*

Eileen R. Tabios and j/j hastain, *the relational elations of ORPHANED ALGEBRA*

Susan Terris, *Ghost of Yesterday, Natural Defenses*

Madeline Tiger, *Birds of Sorrow and Joy*

Harriet Zinnes, *New and Selected Poems, Weather Is Whether, Light Light or the Curvature of the Earth, Whither Nonstopping, Drawing on the Wall*

For more information, please go to: http://www.marshhawkpress.org.